S0-DYV-063

In Turkey

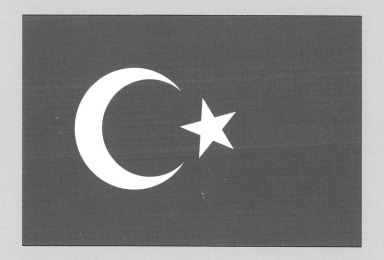

written by **Judy Zocchi** illustrated by **Neale Brodie**

dingles&company New Jersey

For M. Gazi Yasargil

©2005 by Judith Mazzeo Zocchi

All rights reserved.
No part of this book may be reproduced in any form
without written permission from the publishers,
except by a reviewer who may quote brief passages
in a review to be printed in a newspaper or magazine.

First printing

PUBLISHED BY dingles&company
P.O. Box 508 • Sea Girt, New Jersey • 08750
WEBSITE: www.dingles.com • E-MAIL: info@dingles.com

Library of Congress Catalog Card No.: 2004095282
ISBN: 1-59646-031-8

Printed in the United States of America

ART DIRECTION & DESIGN BY Barbie Lambert
ENGLISH EDITED BY Andrea Curley
RESEARCH AND ADDITIONAL COPY WRITTEN BY Robert Neal Kanner
EDUCATIONAL CONSULTANT Bridget Riley Turnbach
ART ASSISTANTS Erin Collity & Sara Sagliano
PRE-PRESS BY Pixel Graphics

The Global Adventures series takes children on an around-the-world exploration of a variety of fascinating countries. The series examines each country's history and physical features as well as its most popular customs, activities, and foods.

Global Adventures

Judy Zocchi

is the author of the Global Adventures, Holiday Happenings, Click & Squeak's Computer Basics, and Paulie and Sasha series. She is a writer and lyricist who holds a bachelor's degree in fine arts/theater from Mount Saint Mary's College and a master's degree in educational theater from New York University. She lives in Manasquan, New Jersey, with her husband, David.

Neale Brodie

is a freelance illustrator who lives in Brighton, England, with his wife and young daughter. He is a self-taught artist, having received no formal education in illustration. As well as illustrating a number of children's books, he has worked as an animator in the computer games industry.

In Turkey TURKISH is what most people speak.

Turkish is the language spoken in Turkey. It is a very ancient language, going back more than 5,500 years ago.

This is my stop.
See you tomorrow.

Covered markets
are called BAZAARS.

A Turkish bazaar is a large marketplace covered
with arched roofs. Shopkeepers sell things such
as rugs, jewelry, souvenirs, clothing, and books.

The **TURKISH LIRA** is what people spend.

New Turkish lira is the currency of Turkey.

KAHVE is served at coffee bars.

Kahve is traditional Turkish coffee. To make it, ground coffee beans are boiled slowly in a long-handled pot called a cezve.

In Turkey children are honored on CHILDREN'S DAY.

Children's Day is celebrated on April 23, the same day as the Republic of Turkey was founded. Mustafa Kemal, the father of modern Turkey, dedicated the day to the children because, he said, "Children are a new beginning of tomorrow."

DOLMA is a vegetable stuffed with rice, nuts, or meat.

Dolma is a popular Turkish dish.

The city of ISTANBUL connects two continents.

Istanbul is an ancient city that was built on two continents. Today, Istanbul has two bridges built over the Bosphorus River, which connect Asia and Europe.

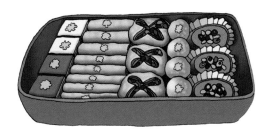

BAKLAVA is a nutty pastry treat.

This centuries-old pastry was a favorite of Turkish sultans. It is made with very thin layers of crisp buttery phyllo dough and honey-sweetened nuts.

In Turkey HAMAM is a Turkish bath.

Hamam is an old Turkish bathing and relaxation custom. It includes spending time in a steam room, massage, soaping, cleansing, and relaxation.

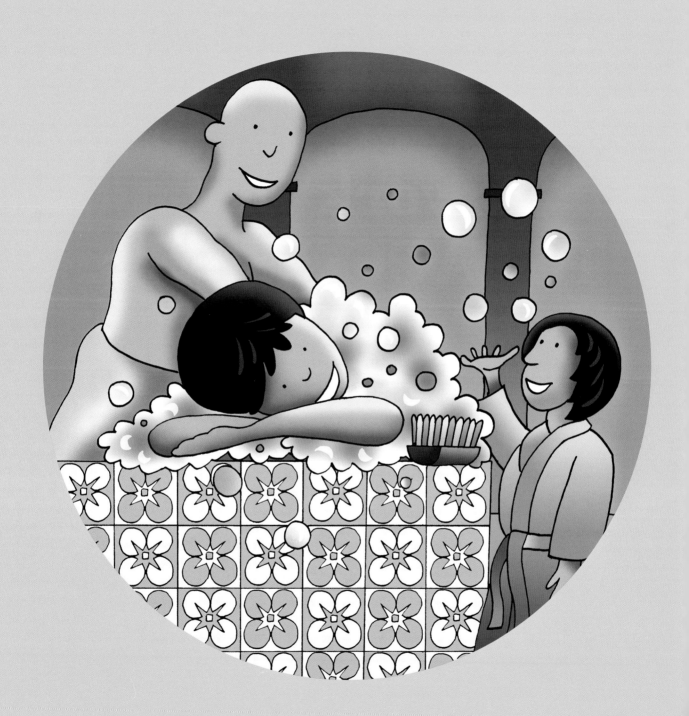

Some people work on TOBACCO farms.

Tobacco growing is an important industry in Turkey. Turkey is the leading producer of oriental tobacco, which is known for its nutty flavor and small leaves.

CAMEL WRESTLING
is a favorite sport.

Camel wrestling is a gentle sport where spectators watch two male camels wrestle, butt, and lean on each other until one runs away.

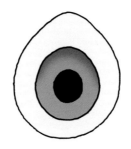

Most households contain "EVIL EYE" charms.

This charm, called the Boncuk, is a blue-colored glass bead that looks like an eye. The charm is supposed to protect one from harm or bad luck.

Turkish culture is fun to learn.

TURKISH

BAZAARS
(BE-zars)

TURKISH LIRA

KAHVE
(kah-ve)

CHILDREN'S DAY

DOLMA
(dol-MAH)

ISTANBUL
(is-tan-BOOL)

BAKLAVA
(BAHK-le-vah)

HAMAM
(hah-MAHM)

TOBACCO

CAMEL WRESTLING

"EVIL EYE"

Canakkale:
This pleasant town in western Turkey is close to the ruins of Troy, the legendary city where the Trojan War was fought in the thirteenth century B.C.E.

Istanbul

Ankara ★

Canakkale

Selcuk

Konya

GREECE

CYPRUS

Selcuk: This small town in western Turkey is near Ephesus, one of the best-preserved cities of ancient times. There you can see many ancient ruins, including the Temple of Diana, one of the largest and greatest temples of its time.

Konya: When visiting this city, don't miss Catalhoyu. This is an archeological excavation site where a settlement dating back 9,000 years was found, making it one of the oldest villages in the world.

GEORGIA

ARM

TURKEY

IRAN

IRAQ

N
W E
S

See what you can discover at every turn!

OFFICIAL NAME:
Republic of Turkey

CAPITAL CITY:
Ankara

CURRENCY:
New Turkish Lira

MAJOR LANGUAGES:
Turkish, Kurdish, Arabic

BORDERS:
Black Sea, Georgia, Armenia,
Azerbaijan, Iran, Iraq, Syria,
Mediterranean Sea, Aegean Sea,
Greece, Bulgaria

CONTINENTS:
Europe and Asia

ABOUT TURKEY

Turkey is a very ancient land. Neanderthal man, the ancestor of modern humans, appeared there almost 300,000 years ago. Over time, many great empires claimed the area as their own, including the Greek and Roman empires. In 1923, Mustafa Kemal, a Turkish World War I hero, founded the Republic of Turkey. The new republic focused on modernizing itself and replaced religious laws with secular, or nonreligious, ones. Today, Turkey is a mix of old and new, with Eastern and Western influences. Its most important industries are manufacturing and exporting textiles and clothing.

UNDERSTANDING AND CELEBRATING CULTURAL DIFFERENCES

- What do you have in common with children from Turkey?
- What things do you do differently from the children in Turkey?
- What is you favorite new thing you learned about Turkey?
- What unique thing about your culture would you like to share?

TRAVELING THROUGH TURKEY

- Turkey is a Middle Eastern country; on what two continents does it lie?
- On which sea is the resort town of Antalya situated?
- What is the name of the mountains in the northern part of the country?

TRY SOMETHING NEW...

Play a Turkish game called Kelebek (Butterfly). It is just like hide and seek except that you turn off all the lights and play in the dark. Choose someone to be the Kelebek. When the Kelebek tags another player, he or she becomes the Kelebek!

For more information on the Global Adventures series or to find activities that coordinate with it, explore our website at **www.dingles.com**.